# NEW HAMPSHIRE

# NEW HAMPSHIRE

The Spirit of America

*Text by Patricia Harris and David Lyon*

## Harry N. Abrams, Inc., Publishers

NEW YORK

This series was originated by Walking Stick Press, San Francisco
Series Designer: Linda Herman; Series Editor: Diana Landau

For Harry N. Abrams, Inc.:
    Project Manager: Ruth A. Peltason
    Editor: Nicole Columbus
    Designer: Ana Rogers

Photo research:
    Laurie Platt Winfrey, Leslie Van Lindt, Van Bucher
    Carousel Research, Inc.

Page 1: Sheep in Andover. *Photo David Brownell*
Page 2: Stone wall near Lake Sunapee. *Photo David Brownell*

**Library of Congress Cataloguing-in-Publication Data**
Harris Patricia.
    New Hampshire : the spirit of America / text by Patricia Harris, David Lyon.
    p.    cm.
    ISBN 0–8109–5571–7
    1. New Hampshire—Miscellanea.    2. New Hampshire—Civilization.
    3. New Hampshire—Civilization—Pictorial works.    4. Arts, American—
    New Hampshire.    I. Lyon, David.    II. Title.    III. Series.
F34.H37    2000
974.2—dc21                                                            99–56048

Harry N. Abrams, Inc.
100 Fifth Avenue
New York, N.Y. 10011
www.abramsbooks.com

Star of Bethlehem quilt. *New Hampshire Historical Society*

# CONTENTS

*Introduction*
**A Pillar Apart** 8

**Stately Symbols** 12

**New Hampshire Milestones** 16

**Picturing the Land** 18
Which Way the Wind Blows 20
The Alps of America 22
Kettles, Potholes, and Basins 24

**Making History** 26
The First Granite Staters 26
Patriots and Pirateers 28
Drawing the Line 30
Reach for the Sky 32

**Commerce and Culture** 34
Rock Farmers and Ice Pickers 34
Creating the Great Escape 36
Before the Mast 40
Mill Town, America 42

**Articles of Faith** 44

**Public Works** 46
Making Tracks 46
Block of Ages 48
Over the River, Through the Woods 50
The Art of Politics 52

**Private Lives**     54
    Portsmouth Privilege     56
    Great Gardeners     59

**Pastimes**     62
    Simple Pleasures     62
    Rev It Up     64

**Lively and Literary Arts**     66
    The MacDowell Colony     66
    *Yankee* Magazine     68
    Lines of Granite     70
    Summer Song and Dance     74

**Saint-Gaudens: Icons in Bronze**     76

**Circles of Friends**     78
    The Cornish Colony     78
    The White Mountain School     80

**Celebrating Crafts**     82

**Recent Visions**     84

**Only in New Hampshire**     86
    Great People and Great Places     88

**New Hampshire by the Seasons**     90
*A Perennial Calendar of Events and Festivals*

**Where to Go**     92
*Museums, Attractions, Gardens, and Other Arts Resources*

*Credits*     95

*New England* by Janice Kasper, 1995. Much of New Hampshire's interior conforms to the New England type: rolling landscape punctuated by a peaked white church, a brick mill, and blocky wooden houses. *Collection Julia B. Leisenring. Photo William Thuss*

*"Live free or die; death is not the worst of evils."*

New Hampshire Revolutionary War hero General John Stark, 1809

New Hampshire is called the Granite State for good reason. It resists exterior pressures as strongly as its granite mountains withstood the abrasive weight of glacial ice sheets. New Hampshire was the first American colony to declare its independence from Britain and the first to write its own state constitution—a document that explicitly asserts the right of revolution. When New Hampshire legislators ratified the U.S. Constitution in 1788, they did so only after a spirited debate and a narrow vote. Then, as now, the issue was self-determination.

This land's commitment to liberty was first and perhaps best expressed by New Hampshire native John Stark, Revolutionary War hero of the Battle of Bennington. He hailed his comrades at their 1809 reunion with a toast that echoes through the ages, and in a flourish of forefather worship the state legislature adopted Stark's "Live Free or Die" as the state motto in 1945. They wedded it to the craggy profile of the Old Man of the Mountain—a granite formation in the White Mountains resembling the profile of a face—and ordered the device emblazoned across every official document concerning recreational, industrial, and agricultural resources. The motto has long graced New Hampshire license plates.

Like its New England seacoast siblings, New Hampshire flourished on the Caribbean trade of the early 18th century, grew fat on the booty of privateering a century later, and kept atop the international marine trade for as long as wood and canvas ruled the waves. Its Portsmouth shipwrights included many fine carvers and joiners, and Portsmouth merchants employed them to build fine houses and fine furniture to fill their rooms.

New Hampshire's White Mountains tower indomitably above the rest of

*The Tilton Family,* attributed to Joseph H. Davis, probably Deerfield, January 1837. *Abby Aldrich Rockefeller Folk Art Center, Williamsburg*

the northeastern U.S., visible from every adjoining state. They signal something a bit aloof about the state's character—a rectitude that stands in splendid isolation. From these mountain slopes flow the rivers that powered New England's looms and stitcheries, and to their summits have climbed generations of seekers, mystics, dreamers, and artists. Although partly tamed by trails, toll road, and cog railway, Mount Washington remains a formidable presence, especially in winter, when its high winds and bitter cold can make Minnesota seem warm.

In 1672, writer John Josselyn denounced the New Hampshire upland as "daunting terrible being full of rocky hills, as thick as Molehills in a Meadow, and cloathed with infinite thick woods." A century and a half later, when the eastern seaboard had been subdued and settled, attitudes had changed. Those hills and woods became emblematic of Nature resplendent, as philosopher Ralph Waldo Emerson and theologian-cum-travel-writer Thomas Starr King taught. The founders of the Hudson River School—Thomas Cole and George Inness among them—sought transporting vistas in the White Mountains. Later in the 19th century, New Hampshire became the great escape, a place where a simple life based on pioneer verities could be experienced amid natural wonders. Scenic tourism quickly became one of the state's enduring industries.

By the end of that century, this popular image of New Hampshire ushered in the era of the art colony. Sunday painters had long pitched their easels at Crawford Notch or above the Flume gorge in Franconia, but now it was official: the most prominent public sculptor of his age, Augustus Saint-Gaudens, gathered around him a coterie of leading intellectual and artistic lights of the late 19th and early 20th centuries in pastoral idyll along the New Hampshire banks of the Connecticut River. The hardscrabble farms, low hills,

*New Hampshire Village* by William Glackens, 1922. New Hampshire's bucolic landscape, laced with rivers and streams, continues to present a nostalgic picture of preindustrial America. *York Gallery*

and tranquil woods of the Monadnock region around Dublin and Peterborough became the quiet rage of artists, writers, and musicians—all the more so when the MacDowell Colony was born in 1907.

New Hampshire cultivates that retreat from modern life, popping out once every four years like a groundhog to predict the presidential weather, and then ducking away until the next round of candidates comes stumping. Its small towns and villages are comely, quiet places where artisans and artists work apace. Poet Maxine Kumin raises riding horses and schools the canter of her verse between the lakes and the mountains, while J. D. Salinger haunts Cornish, a silent literary legend whose neighbors guard his privacy. In dozens of communities, potters and weavers and tapestry stitchers go about their crafts, making and remaking New England home fashion and passing on their skills to younger artisans. But for all its plainspoken rectitude, there is warmth at the heart of New Hampshire. As Cornelius Weygandt wrote in the New Hampshire volume of the American Guide series in 1938, "It is granite that holds longest after nightfall the heat of the sun." ❄

## NEW HAMPSHIRE

*"The Granite State"*
*9th State*

*Date of Statehood*
JUNE 12, 1788

*Capital*
CONCORD

*Bird*
PURPLE FINCH

*Flower*
PURPLE LILAC

*Tree*
WHITE BIRCH

*Animal*
WHITE-TAILED DEER

*Amphibian*
SPOTTED NEWT

*Wildflower*
PINK LADY'S SLIPPER

*Rock*
GRANITE

**Purple finch and purple lilac**

In 1931 New Hampshire's legislature overhauled the 156-year-old state seal to create an unequivocal image of stalwart character and patriotism. The current seal shows a granite boulder—symbolic of the state's rugged terrain and citizenry—and a broadside view of the frigate *Raleigh*, built in Portsmouth in 1776 and the first vessel to carry the new American flag into battle. The official emblem, a profile view of the Old Man of the Mountain, appears often in state literature. Other New Hampshire symbols balance native resources with the contributions of settlers. The white birch is honored as the state tree, in part because Native Americans used it to make canoes. The state flower, the purple lilac, was imported from England and introduced to the colonies in plantings at the home of Governor Benning Wentworth in 1750. The legislators settled on the lilac as

# "Live Free or Die"

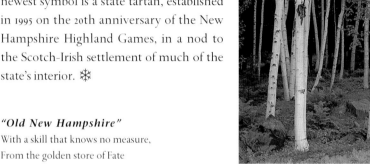

State motto

"symbolic of that hardy character of the men and women of the Granite State." The newest symbol is a state tartan, established in 1995 on the 20th anniversary of the New Hampshire Highland Games, in a nod to the Scotch-Irish settlement of much of the state's interior. ❈

## *"Old New Hampshire"*

With a skill that knows no measure,
From the golden store of Fate
God, in His great love and wisdom,
Made the rugged Granite State;
Made the lakes, the fields, the forests;
Made the Rivers and the rills;
Made the bubbling, crystal fountains
of New Hampshire's Granite Hills
*Refrain:*
Old New Hampshire, Old New Hampshire
Old New Hampshire Grand and Great
We will sing of Old New Hampshire,
Of the dear old Granite State

*Words by Dr. John F. Holmes, music by Maurice Hoffman, Jr., 1926. "Old New Hampshire" is the official state song; there are eight other honorary state songs.*

*Above:* After the evergreen forest of New Hampshire was largely felled in the 19th century, it was succeeded by a hardwood forest of maples, oaks, and the state tree, the white birch. *Photo Jim Zipp/Photo Researchers. Left:* Pink lady's slipper (*Cypripedium acaule*), the state wildflower. *Photo Rod Planck/Photo Researchers*

## Maple Oatmeal Cookies

Like other New England states, New Hampshire is a major producer of maple syrup.

1 cup unbleached flour
1 tsp. baking powder
¼ tsp. salt
1 cup rolled oats
½ cup chopped walnuts
½ cup shortening
2 eggs
¾ cup maple syrup
½ tsp. vanilla

Sift flour, baking powder, and salt into a large bowl. Add oats and walnuts, mix well and set aside. Cream shortening in a medium bowl, add eggs, and beat until light and fluffy. Stir in maple syrup and vanilla. Pour into the dry ingredients and mix well. Drop by tablespoonfuls onto greased cookie sheets; bake in a preheated 400° F oven for 12 minutes. Makes about 48.

A Collection of Maple Recipes, *New Hampshire Maple Producers Association, Londonderry*

## A Symbol Goes Astray

The frigate *Raleigh,* featured on the state seal, had a checkered career. Built in Portsmouth in 1776, she was unable to go to sea for 15 months for lack of armament; when she finally sailed to France for munitions, her captain was dismissed for incompetence. Run aground off Maine, she was captured by the British and used against the Americans for the rest of the Revolutionary War. The British Navy so liked the *Raleigh's* sturdiness that they used her as a model for other battle frigates.

White-tailed deer abound in fields bordering New Hampshire woodlands. *Photo Stephen J. Krasemann/Photo Researchers*

## Unique Observances

Around the time other New England states were abolishing **Fast Day**—a traditional day of prayer and fasting inherited from the Puritans—New Hampshire made the archaic holiday law, in 1899. Usually observed on the last Thursday in April, it was moved in 1949 to the fourth Monday in April, guaranteeing a three-day weekend at a good time for cleaning rain gutters. Fast Day was abolished in 1991 in favor of Civil Rights Day, itself replaced in 1999 by Martin Luther King, Jr. Day. Also in 1899, the governor launched **Old Home Week** to encourage erstwhile Granite State families who had migrated west to visit their ancestral stomps. Traditionally the third week of August, the observation has dwindled to a weekend celebration with local pageants and picnics.

*Left:* Red-spotted newts, the state amphibian. *Photo E. R. Degginger/Photo Researchers. Above:* The madcap call of the common loon echoes across many New Hampshire lakes on summer nights, making this handsome waterfowl a beloved unofficial symbol of the state. *Photo David Brownell*

**c. 8000 B.C.** First inhabitants of region hunt large mammals along the now-submerged coastal shelf. Some evidence of chert mining for tool material in White Mountains.

**1603** Captain Martin Pring explores the Piscataqua River near Portsmouth for England.

**1605** Explorer Samuel de Champlain enters Piscataqua Bay.

**1614** Captain John Smith sails along New Hampshire coast.

**1623** First settlements established at Odiorne Point near Portsmouth and at Dover on Piscataqua River.

**1633** First town government in New Hampshire is established at Dover. First church in New Hampshire is built the following year.

**1642** Darby Field ascends Mt. Washington with two Indian guides.

**1673** Nashua, the first interior town, is settled.

**1756** *New Hampshire Gazette,* state's first newspaper, published at Portsmouth.

**1765** Conway is first town chartered in the White Mountains region.

**1769** Dartmouth College in Hanover chartered.

**1770** First colonial settlement on Lake Winnipesaukee at Alton Bay.

**1774** Colonists capture British supplies from Fort William and Mary in Newcastle in the first act of insurrection of Revolutionary War.

**1776** New Hampshire adopts first written state constitution and declares independence.

**1777** Vermont declares independence from New Hampshire to create a separate republic.

**1788** New Hampshire becomes ninth state to ratify U.S. Constitution, thereby putting the federal Union into effect.

**1803** First hotel in White Mountains opens.

**1815** Frigate *Washington* is first ship completed at Portsmouth Naval Shipyard.

**1819** State capitol building completed in Concord.

**1819** Power loom introduced at Amoskeag Mills in Manchester.

**1820** State historical society founded; one of the oldest in the U.S.

**1833** Free public library established in Peterborough; oldest continuously tax-supported library in the U.S.

**1833** Steamboat service begins on Lake Winnipesaukee.

**1847** New Hampshire establishes first U.S. 10-hour workday for factory workers.

**1852** First hotel built on the summit of Mt. Washington.

**1853** Franklin Pierce, born in Hillsborough, inaugurated as 14th U.S. president.

**1853** Republican Party founded as an anti-slavery party, in Exeter.

**1859** First steamboat, *Surprise,* launched on Lake Sunapee.

**1861** Carriage Road to summit of Mt. Washington opens.

**1875** First summer hotel built on Lake Sunapee at Burkehaven.

**1881** First organized summer boys' camp opens on Squam Lake.

**1902** Construction of Mount Washington Hotel marks the conclusion of the golden age of White Mountains hotel building.

**1905** Treaty ending Russo-Japanese War signed in Portsmouth.

**1908** Mt. Washington Carriage Road opens to automobiles.

**1911** White Mountain National Forest created.

**1913** New Hampshire Old Home Week, third week of August, voted into law.

**1923** New Hampshire College of Agriculture and Mechanic Arts becomes the University of New Hampshire.

**1929** Currier Gallery of Art in Manchester opens.

**1937** Cannon Mountain Aerial Tramway opens.

**1940** M/S *Mount Washington* begins cruises on Lake Winnipesaukee.

**1944** U.N. Monetary and Financial Conference at Bretton Woods creates international fund and bank.

**1946** William Loeb buys *Manchester Union Leader,* the only statewide newspaper; begins publishing ultraconservative editorials on front page.

**1950** New Hampshire Turnpike opens.

**1952** New Hampshire establishes first-in-nation presidential primary elections.

**1958** Strawbery Banke formed to preserve Portsmouth's historic neighborhood.

**1963** New Hampshire becomes first state to legalize a state-run lottery in 20th century.

**1964** Saint-Gaudens National Historic Site established.

**1965** Strawbery Banke Museum opens.

**1980** Sherman Adams Building opens on the summit of Mt. Washington as visitors center and house observatory.

**1984** Hood Museum of Art opens at Dartmouth College in Hanover.

**1990** After 15 years of controversy, Seabrook Station becomes last nuclear power plant licensed in U.S.

**1995** Museum of New Hampshire History opens in Concord.

**1999** New Hampshire featured at Folklife Festival at Smithsonian Institution in Washington, D.C.

Fall leaves. *Photo David Brownell*

New Hampshire is a land of rock and crag, where a glacially etched landscape surrounds a ribcage of rocky-top mountains. Thousands of rivulets run off these hills, feeding the state's three great river systems. The valley of the Connecticut River, forming the boundary with Vermont, is New Hampshire's cropland. Bisecting the state south of the mountains, the Merrimack with its *pawtucket* falls provided industrial muscle. And the Androscoggin served as a highway to the sea for the north country's tall timber. The 18-mile coast of slate ledges and sandy beaches could be a footnote to Granite State geography—except that its sole harbor of Portsmouth has long been New Hampshire's storefront on the world.

The ungenerous nature of New Hampshire soils has discouraged development, leaving most of the land covered in natural habitat of pine forest and spruce swamp—a world better suited to moose and bear, bittern and grouse than to agriculture. The farmer's loss has been the naturalist's gain, making New Hampshire by nature a refuge and retreat from the whirl and whorl of modern life. ❄

Here in purgatory bare ground
is visible, except in shady places
where snow prevails.

Still, each day sees
the restoration of another animal:
a sparrow, just now a sleepy wasp;
and, at twilight, the skunk
pokes out of the den,
anxious for mates and meals. . . .

*Jane Kenyon, from "Mud Season" in*
Otherwise: New & Selected Poems, *1996*

*The River at Ascutney* **by Maxfield Parrish, 1942. Parrish was one of the first—and the last—members of the Cornish colony, working there until his death in 1966. Known for his early advertising art and book illustrations, he primarily painted landscapes after the 1930s.** *Art Shows and Products, New York. Photo courtesy Archives of the American Illustrators Gallery, New York*

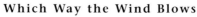

## Which Way the Wind Blows

New Hampshire is famous for weather prognosticators. Scribes at the *Old Farmer's Almanac* in Dublin use a formula devised in 1792 to make educated guesses a full year ahead, factoring in sunspot cycles and meteorological data as a nod to modern science. The *OFA* contends that "there is a cause-and-effect pattern to all phenomena, thus making long-range weather forecasts possible," yet concedes that "neither we nor anyone else has as yet gained sufficient insight into the mysteries of the universe to predict weather with anything resembling total accuracy."

Observational science is the goal on Mount Washington's summit, where the first winter weather station was established in 1870–71. The observers clocked a wind of 92 mph and estimated stronger gusts, but didn't dare step outside to retrieve their instruments. In 1932, the modern Mount Washington Observatory debuted to keep an eye on the storms, which it still does under the National Weather Service. On August 12, 1934, observers recorded a gust of 231 mph, the strongest wind ever measured on earth. The station also conducts research in high-altitude physics and low-temperature technology, testing everything from jet engines to long johns to paint for use in polar climes.

*Above:* The frost-rimed weather observatory on Mount Washington records some of the harshest weather reported in the lower 48 states. *Courtesy Mt. Washington Observatory. Top left: The Old Farmer's Almanac, published by Yankee Publications, remains the most widely consulted of long-range weather forecasts. Photo Doug Mindell*

*Sun Setting onto Fog* by Wolf Kahn, 1992. Strong temperature extremes and changeable weather in the New Hampshire lakes region produces unusual meteorological effects, including fog at the end of the day when a cold front moves in. *Beadleston Gallery, New York, N.Y. ©Wolf Kahn/ Licensed by VAGA, N.Y.*

"NEW YORK HAS PEOPLE, THE NORTHWEST rain, Iowa soybeans, and Texas money. New Hampshire has weather and seasons. Convention speaks merely of four seasons; here, we number at least a thousand, and on one good day our spendthrift climate runs through seven or eight."

*Donald Hall,* Here at Eagle Pond, *1990*

## Chilled Out

Because Mount Washington juts into a major North American storm track, the summit experiences some of the most severe weather outside the polar regions. Average annual temperature is 26.9° F, with February averaging 5° F. The record low was -47° F in January 1934. In February 1969, 172.8 inches of snow fell, 49.3 inches in a single 24-hour period. Wind on the summit reaches hurricane force, 75 mph, 104 days per year on average. The summit also endures fog an average of 305 days per year—some 430 fog-bound hours per month.

*Artists Sketching in the White Mountains* by Winslow Homer, 1868. Although Homer was more at home on the sea, he sometimes joined the crowds of landscape painters using North Conway as their base in the mid- and late-19th century. *Portland Museum of Art*

## The Alps of America

When explorer Giovanni da Verrazano sailed the New England coast in 1524, he noted in his log "high mountains within the land." Indeed, the White Mountains are New England's most prominent geographic feature, visible on a clear day from Cape Cod, Massachusetts, and the Adirondacks of New York. The White Mountains may lack the towering height of the Rockies, having endured an additional 260 million years of erosion, but their abrupt rise from sea level reminded European observers of the Alps. With 48 peaks above 4,000 feet, the White Mountain group covers more than 1,200 square miles, mostly in north-central New Hampshire. Above the tree line, these rocky balds are dotted with sedges and lichens, bursting forth suddenly with alpine gardens of glacial relict wildflowers.

The tallest section of the Whites is the group of peaks known as the Presidential Range—so named in 1820, when New Hampshire's secretary of state and his party climbed their heights and christened peaks for presidents Adams, Jefferson, Madison, and Monroe, reserving "Washington" for the tallest of them all—6,228 feet.

". . . IT IS TOWARD MT. WASHINGTON THAT THE TOURIST TURNS obediently, the cynosure of all eyes. How many a little hill in New Hampshire and Vermont basks in the reflected glory of being a 'Mt. Washington look-out!'"

*Brooks Atkinson and W. Kent Olson,*
New England's White Mountains: At Home in the Wild, *1978*

## What Is a Notch?

The White Mountains do not quite form an impenetrable wall. Scattered among the ridges and peaks are nine deep defiles that New Englanders call "notches." Comparable to the "gaps" of other American mountain chains, these U-shaped passages are once-sharp river valleys smoothed and flattened by the pressures of the Pleistocene ice sheet.

*Above:* The granite profile of the Old Man of the Mountain has come to symbolize the rugged New Hampshire spirit. *Photo David Brownell.* *Left:* Mount Washington and other high ridges in the Presidential Range are home to a number of alpine plants, including Lapland rosebay. *Photo Jim Zipp/Photo Researchers*

Fall color, Monadnock region. *Photo David Brownell. Opposite left:* Squam Lake starred as the title location in the 1981 film *On Golden Pond.* Katharine Hepburn and Henry Fonda both won Oscars for their performances as the aging couple who have come to greet the loons. *Photofest. Opposite right:* Squam Lake, viewed here from Rattlesnake Overlook, is typical of the glacial lakes in the New Hampshire highlands. *Photo David Brownell*

### Kettles, Potholes, and Basins

The glacier-carved face of New Hampshire is dotted with lakes and ponds, some 273 of them cradled between the southern flank of the White Mountains and a line of bumpy drumlins. Many are little more than glacial kettle ponds, where big chunks of ice broke off the receding ice sheets and melted in place. Others are drowned valleys, of which the largest is the 72-square-mile Lake Winnipesaukee—a summer playground of motor boats and water-skiers, dotted with hundreds of islands and lined with summer camps on its 186-mile shore. An Algonquian word that real-estate agents and tourism promoters translate as "beautiful water in a high place" (and anthropologists translate as "pouring-out place

where the fish are"), "Winnipesaukee" had 132 recorded spellings until the state legislature enshrined the current one as law in 1931.

In all, lakes and ponds cover nearly 20 percent of New Hampshire's surface, providing vacation retreats for people and critical habitat for waterfowl, including loons, scoters, goldeneyes, canvasbacks, and mergansers.

AS LATE AS YESTERDAY ICE PREOCCUPIED
the pond—dark, half-melted, waterlogged.
Then it sank in the night, one piece,
taking winter with it. And afterward
everything seems simple and good.

*Jane Kenyon, from "Ice Out" in*
Otherwise: New & Selected Poems, *1996*

*Indian Hunter with Bow* by Anna Elizabeth Lancaster Hobbs, c. 1840. Although most Native Americans had left New Hampshire by 1800, they remained a powerful symbol of the wilderness in popular art. *Hood Museum of Art, Dartmouth College. Opposite left: A College in the Wilderness.* Founded in 1768 by Eleazor Wheelock, Dartmouth College lay on the northwestern frontier of New England civilization. *American Heritage Publishing Company*

### The First Granite Staters

When the first European settlers built homes and planted crops at the mouth of the Piscataqua River in 1623, New Hampshire was thinly settled by Algonquian peoples of three groups. The Penacook Confederacy of tribes occupied the fertile banks of the Merrimack River and the productive marshlands of the seacoast. Sokoki bands farmed the shores and fished the waters of Lakes Winnipesaukee and Ossipee, while the Coosucs tended their corn, beans, and pumpkins in the green intervales of the upper Connecticut River valley. Nomadic in varying degrees, they all followed the hunting–fishing pattern of Eastern Woodland tribes.

The charismatic leader of the Penacook Confederacy, Passaconaway, counseled peaceful relations with European settlers, but in 1675 his grandson, Kancamagus, led the tribes against the settlers during King Philip's War with disastrous results. The surviving Penacooks and most of the Sokokis fled north to join the St. Francis nation in Quebec. The 18th-century French and Indian War decimated the Coosucs, who sided with the French. Yet when Dartmouth College was founded in 1768, it was "for the education & instruction of Youth of the Indian Tribes" —and, almost parenthetically, "and also of English Youth and any others."

*Dartmouth University, 1803* by George Ticknor, c. 1803. Although much augmented by newer buildings, Dartmouth and its green remain the center of Hanover. *Hood Museum of Art, Dartmouth College*

## The Death of Chocorua

New Hampshire lore tells of Chocorua, a survivor of a 1725 massacre, who entrusted his motherless son to settler Cornelius Campbell. When the boy was accidentally poisoned, Chocorua slaughtered the white family in a grief-stricken rage and fled to a mountaintop where Campbell hunted him down. Before he expired from gunshot wounds (and falling off the mountain), the dying "savage" proclaimed, "Chocorua goes to the Great Spirit—his curse stays with the white man!" This romantic parable captured public imagination: the peak was dubbed Mount Chocorua and Thomas Cole's painting, *The Death of Chocorua,* was critically acclaimed.

*General John Stark Running the Gauntlet after Capture by the St. Francis Indians by Henry W. Herrick, 1876. New Hampshire's greatest soldier of the French and Indian Wars and the American Revolution, Stark entered the realm of legend in the 19th century. Herrick's watercolor depicts an incident in the French and Indian Wars. Manchester Historic Association*

New Hampshire was first to pick a fight with the English king in the American Revolution. On December 15, 1774, some 400 members of the Portsmouth Sons of Liberty marched over the bridge to New Castle island in Portsmouth harbor and surrounded Fort William and Mary. The commander, caught with just five guards at the fort, surrendered, and the rebels seized a large cache of gunpowder and arms, later issued to American troops at the Battle of Bunker Hill.

Once war broke out, New Hampshire was the only state of the original 13 where no battles took place. But the First N.H. Regiment served continuously on every front for eight years and eight months—probably the longest service record of any Revolutionary regiment. Portsmouth's strategic location on the shipping lanes made it a center of legalized piracy throughout the war, as former merchants armed their ships to the teeth and began to seize British ships for trial and auction at home. So many Portsmouth sailors were engaged in the activity that the Continental Navy could not meet its recruitment quota in New Hampshire. Patriotism was profitable, establishing the fortunes of many a prominent Portsmouth family. When the War of 1812 broke out, Portsmouth reverted to its old ways, again becoming the terror of the British merchant fleet. ❄

*John Paul Jones Shooting a Sailor*, lithograph of a painting by John Collett. Early in his sailing career, before adding "Jones" to his name, merchant captain John Paul ordered an insubordinate sailor flogged. When the man died some weeks later, Paul was cleared by a court of inquiry. At another point, Paul was attacked by a drunken sailor in his cabin and ran the man through with a sword. During the Revolution, British propagandists claimed that the captain—admiral of the American Navy—was a severe disciplinarian who killed his own crew. *Library of Congress*

Federal courts finally settled on the Connecticut River as the boundary between New Hampshire and Vermont, but extended New Hampshire's boundaries to the western bank of the river. *Photo Frank Siteman/Stock Boston*

## Drawing the Line

Carving New Hampshire out of a maze of conflicting land grants took more than three centuries. The king of England settled some of the earliest disputes, giving 28 "Massachusetts" towns along the Merrimack River to New Hampshire in 1740 but rejecting New Hampshire's dubious claims to Vermont and fixing their boundary at the Connecticut River in 1764. New Hampshire's quibbles with Canada resulted in the "Indian Stream War." The treaty ending the American Revolution had set the border with Quebec at the northwestern source of the Connecticut River. Opinions differed on which stream was the source, and both countries claimed the fertile lands of Indian Stream. In 1832, the 300 disgusted residents seceded and founded a minirepublic: the United Inhabitants of Indian Stream Territory. U.S. troops quelled this insurrection, and Daniel Webster won back the territory for his native state in

the 1842 Webster-Ashburton Treaty with Britain. Boundary disputes continued until 1934, when the U.S. Supreme Court set the New Hampshire–Vermont line at the low-water mark of the Connecticut River's west bank. New Hampshire got more land—and the bill for maintaining the bridges!

*Portrait of Daniel Webster ("Black Dan") by Francis Alexander, 1835. Hood Museum of Art, Dartmouth College*

### Daniel Webster, Expatriate

Abraham Lincoln is said to have remarked that New Hampshire, like Maryland, was a good place to have come from. Perhaps he had Daniel Webster in mind. Born in Salisbury to modest means, Webster attended Dartmouth College and represented New Hampshire in the House of Representatives from 1813–16 before quitting to practice law in Boston. But his charisma sent Webster back to Washington, where he rose to fame as the fiery orator of the U.S. Senate—the gentleman from Massachusetts.

**Born to a humble estate, Daniel Webster eventually grew into a country gentleman.**
*Private collection*

**M**ost Granite Staters keep both feet firmly on the ground, but some have had higher aspirations. Thaddeus S. C. Lowe, born in Randolph (now Riverton) in 1832, was passionately devoted to the development of balloons, making his first ascents in 1858. When the Civil War began in 1861, Lowe demonstrated how the balloon could be used as an aerial observation platform by sending the first telegram from the sky to earth through his tether cable. He became Military Aeronaut of the Union Army in the East, building five balloons that rose to 2,500 feet to watch troop movements. Using another novel technology, Lowe also made aerial photographs to guide Union commanders. ❊

*Above:* Professor Thaddeus Lowe observes the battle of Fair Oaks, Virginia, for the Union Army from his balloon the *Intrepid. Corbis-Bettmann. Right:* Lowe makes a balloon ascent to reconnoiter the battlefield at Vienna, Virginia, for Union troops. *Corbis-Bettmann*

# "I touch the future—I teach."

*Christa McAuliffe's motto*

## The New Frontier

The first American in space was Alan B. Shepard, Jr., from Derry. A Korean War and military test pilot, Shepard was a charter Mercury astronaut and made the first suborbital flight on May 5, 1961. New Hampshire answered NASA's call again when Christa McAuliffe, a high school social studies teacher in Concord, won a nationwide teacher-in-space contest. Tragically, the space shuttle *Challenger* exploded 73 seconds after take-off on January 6, 1986, killing McAuliffe and six other crew members. Her work to inspire youth continues at the Christa McAuliffe Planetarium in Concord.

*Above:* Concord high school teacher Christa McAuliffe, the first participant in the teacher-in-space program, perished aboard the space shuttle *Challenger* on January 6, 1986. *Left:* Best known as the first American astronaut to escape earth's gravity and soar briefly into space on the first Mercury launch in 1961, Alan Shepard, who died in 1998, also was one of just 12 men to walk on the moon: during the Apollo 14 mission in February 1971. *Both, NASA/Corbis-Bettmann*

*Plowing the Fields* by William Zorach, 1917. The intervales just east of the Connecticut River historically proved some of New Hampshire's most fertile farmland. *Currier Gallery of Art, Manchester*

### Rock Farmers and Ice Pickers

Despite its stony, stingy soils, New Hampshire has always been a farming state. Colonial settlers felled trees and uprooted boulders, planting in their stead wheat and corn as well as beans, beets, carrots, cabbage, and pumpkins. When Scotch-Irish immigrants to Derry introduced the potato in 1719, the undemanding crop took the region by storm, and the state's agriculture—and cuisine—was transformed. But stones have always been the most prolific harvest on New England farms. Pragmatic farmers piled them up, believing that "good fences make good neighbors," as Derry schoolteacher-poet Robert Frost observed. Building a stone wall was an art, for local wisdom held that it must be "pig-tight, bull-strong and horse-high."

When fields lay fallow beneath the snow, New Hampshire became an icebox for the world. Its ponds contributed heavily to the 146,000 tons shipped out of Boston in 1856 to places as far away as Australia and China. The broad expanse of Lake Winnipesaukee became cold-country gold; in 1890–91, half a million tons of Winnipesaukee ice worth $2 million were harvested, much of it shipped to the domestic market by rail. When Yankee ice met carbonated beverage, the classic "ice cream soda" was born.

*Above:* New Hampshire's lakes and ponds yielded a good annual harvest of ice for refrigeration. *New Hampshire Historical Society. Left: Burnap Homestead* by Florence Lee Wilson, 1894. The classic New Hampshire farm features long stone walls and farmhouse buildings, one attached to another after centuries of expansion. *Phyllis Randall Collection*

"AGRICULTURE IS, AND ALWAYS WILL BE, THE CHIEF BUSINESS OF THE people of New Hampshire, if they attend to their true interest. Every tree which is felled in the forest opens to the sun a new spot of earth, which with cultivation, will produce food for man and beast."

*Rev. Jeremy Belknap,* The History of New Hampshire, *1792*

The forest roads and mountain trails of the White Mountains were firmly established as recreational assets soon after the Civil War. With the arrival of inexpensive rail service to the region in the 1880s, walking the Whites became a common getaway, even for factory workers from metropolitan New England. *New Hampshire Historical Society*

## Resorts and Retreats

The difficulty of farming its land ultimately proved New Hampshire's economic salvation: much of its natural beauty remained pristine until entrepreneurs learned how to make money from it. Wolfeboro, on Lake Winnipesaukee, justifiably calls itself "America's first summer resort." In 1768, colonial governor John Wentworth built the first grand summer estate here and ordered a 45-mile road built from Portsmouth to his front door. Wealthy Portsmouth merchants followed suit, and within 50 years, New Hampshire lakes were ringed with summer getaways. As farmers migrated west after the mid-19th century, many Bostonians and New Yorkers snapped up failed farms at bargain prices to turn into pastoral retreats.

## Summer Idylls and Scenic Wonders

Down-to-earth Granite Staters were amused and astonished when, around 1820, the mountain inns set up to house teamsters driving freight from coast to north country began to host a more refined class of visitors. They were the first Scenic Tourists, inspired by Romantic notions of the sublime and convinced that contemplation of natural wonders could illuminate their souls. Among them were Ralph Waldo Emerson and his circle, including Henry David Thoreau and Nathaniel Hawthorne. Hawthorne's notebook lists his hotel companions in 1832 as a doctor, a geologist, two newlywed couples from Massachusetts, a pair of Georgia gentlemen, and a young man with opera glasses and a penchant for spouting Byronic verse about the glories of mountain scenery.

Tourists on the porch of a rustic camp in the White Mountains, n.d.
*Culver Pictures*

The Mount Washington Hotel & Resort, built in 1902, was the last of the grand White Mountains resort hotels to be constructed and is one of only two that still stand. *Mt. Washington Hotel & Resort*

## Bringing the Masses to the Mountain

If genteel folk wanted to behold the sublime, practical Granite Staters were happy to oblige. The rugged summit of Mount Washington, tallest peak in the Northeast, had "sublime" to spare, and the curiously human visage of the Old Man of the Mountain at Franconia Notch could set Romantic minds reeling. Between 1850 and 1900, resort hotels proliferated in the White Mountains like daisies on a June hillside. Only the Mount Washington Hotel and The Balsams survive from those halcyon days.

Early scenic tourists hiked or rode horses up Mount Washington, but technology soon gave them a lift. When Sylvester

Marsh hatched the idea of building a cog railway to the summit, one state legislator likened the idea to building a railroad to the moon—but Marsh laughed last when the Cog Railway began operating in 1869. The more prosaic Carriage Road to the summit opened first, in 1861, as the world's first mountain toll road. Both railway and road remain the most popular ways to ascend Mount Washington.

The Mount Washington Cog Railroad was considered a pipe dream when first proposed in the 1850s, but it has provided regular service to the summit since 1869. *Photo Jim Zipp/Photo Researchers*

"MEN PUT OUT SIGNS REPRESENTING THEIR DIFFERENT TRADES; jewelers hang out a monster watch; shoemakers, a huge boot; and, up in Franconia, God Almighty has hung out a sign that in New England He makes men."

*Benjamin Willey,* Incidents in White Mountain History, *1856*

## Depth of Field

Seven years after Oliver Wendell Holmes invented the stereopticon, the Keystone View Co. was founded in Littleton and immediately struck gold with 3-D views of the White Mountains. The company also featured its neighbors in the first strip-style minidramas, comedies, and tragedies. Before closing in 1909, Keystone published more than 100,000 scenes from around the world.

*Picking up the Pilot—Isle of Shoals, New Hampshire* by James E. Butterworth, n.d. Merchant ship meets with pilot boat to thread the channel between Isles of Shoals and Portsmouth harbor. The two boats are just south of Smuttynose Island, about 100 yards from the marine border with Maine. *Christie's Images. Below: Ship Launching* by Herbert Waters, 1955. *McGowan Fine Art*

## Before the Mast

Blessed with a calm harbor and a river that could deliver towering mast pines from the northern forest, Portsmouth evolved a busy shipbuilding trade, constructing everything from fishing ketches to 19th-century clipper ships. The local claim to fame was the frigate *Ranger,* built on Badger's Island in 1777 for Commodore John Paul Jones and the first ship to fly the new American flag.

After the Revolution, the Portsmouth Naval Shipyard was established on neighboring Dennett's Island; its first vessel, the 74-gun frigate *Washington,* slid down the ways in July 1815. The shipyard—mostly on the Maine side of the harbor—produced many naval vessels for the Civil War and Spanish-American War. Today its primary role is to outfit and recondition submarines.

# Westward Ho!

Even as New Hampshire–born Horace Greeley exhorted "Go west, young man!" in his New York newspaper, a tiny Concord firm made its fortune by helping Americans do just that. The Abbott, Downing Company built wagons in which thousands of pioneers crossed the prairies, while making its name chiefly with the Concord Coach—vehicle of choice for cross-country stage lines as well as for elegant urban hotels. First offered in 1825, the coach had a flat roof to carry luggage, sturdy hardwood construction, and a cowhide brace suspension to ease the bumps. Mark Twain dubbed it "an imposing cradle on wheels."

E. Putnam & Co. used this Concord Coach to service the Glens Falls, Lake George, and Chester, N.Y., area, transporting passengers to and from large resort hotels. The Concord Coach was the most elegant and practical long-distance transportation of its day. While it was used as a luxury conveyance by Eastern hotels, it set the standard for gracious travel in the newly opened American West. *University of New Hampshire*

## Mill Town, America

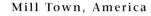

Streams and rivers draining the White Mountains form a web across southern and central New Hampshire, and during the 19th century most such waterways were harnessed to operate textile and leather mills. Nowhere did the water-powered mill dominate life more than in Manchester, where an 1805 mill grew into the world's largest cotton-mill complex before its precipitous decline after 1922. Named for the powerful Amoskeag Falls on the Merrimack River, the Amoskeag Manufacturing Company was the king of gingham, at its height turning out a mile of cloth per minute of the workday. Given inadequate Yankee labor, Amoskeag recruited throughout Quebec, thereby transforming Manchester into a Franco-American enclave. Another textile-driven town was Keene; its Faulkner & Colony Company, founded in 1815, dominated American production of cotton flannel, producing 27-inch-wide bolts in primary colors. Red was favored for shirts of the Forty-niners; its blue flannel was the uniform of New Orleans stevedores.

This mid-19th-century view of Manchester's Amoskeag Mills shows a sprawling series of mills along the city's industrial canal. By the Civil War it was the largest textile mill complex in the world. *Manchester Historic Association*

"THE AMOSKEAG MANUFACTURING COMPANY WAS GARGANTUAN. . . .
Each mill if placed on end would be a skyscraper."

*Boyden Sparks,* Saturday Evening Post, *1936*

*Coming out of the Amoskeag Manufacturing Company* by Lewis Hine, 1909. Child labor laws came late to New Hampshire, and children as young as 12 still labored in the textile mills when Hine took this photograph at 6 p.m. on May 24, 1909. *Library of Congress*

## Showpiece Mills

With only a handful of specialty mills still operating, the textile mill is history in New Hampshire, but three communities preserve their heritage as tourist attractions. Harrisville claims to be one of the most perfectly preserved mill towns in New England. Frye's Measure Mill in Wilton, built in 1858 and now making Shaker boxes and trays, is America's only remaining water-powered mill. Belknap Mill in Laconia, once a hotbed of the hosiery industry, is the oldest unaltered brick textile mill in the country.

*Factories, Portsmouth, New Hampshire* by Stefan Hirsch, 1930. Although manufacturing was never central to Portsmouth's economy, the city had some shoe factories and a button factory in the early 20th century until the destructive floods of 1936. *Courtesy SBC Communications, Inc.*

Congregationalism was practically New Hampshire's state religion until 1819, when the Toleration Act ended taxpayer support of churches. But a range of sects won many converts. Quakers settled in Dover in the 1680s and formed a third of the population by 1800; their graceful 1768 meetinghouse remains in use. Doomsday-cult followers of William Miller were numerous, though their fervor faded when Armageddon did not arrive on October 22, 1844. The Mormon faith flourished in the 1830s and 1840s. Brigham Young was preaching in Peterborough when he was called to lead the church on Joseph Smith's sudden death, and 136 Peterborough citizens followed him to Salt Lake City—including his 13th wife. The pragmatic mystics of American faith, the Shakers, settled in Canterbury and Enfield in the 1790s. Brother David Parker of Canterbury

bury invented an industrial washing machine in 1858, and the community manufactured and sold them to resort hotels as far south as Florida. The Canterbury Shakers were the first people in New Hampshire with electric lights, maintained their own telephone system, and owned (communally, of course) some of New Hampshire's first automobiles. The Enfield and Canterbury Shaker villages are now museums. ❋

The Shakers of Canterbury were among the first rural communities in New Hampshire to boast telephone service and electric lights. *Canterbury Shaker Village*

"AT FIRST THIS SHAKER DRIVE FOR PERFECTION SEEMED KIND OF dangerous to me, because I was far from perfect myself, but I soon learned that I needn't have worried. . . . Shakers like Lillian and Bertha were interested in improving their own behavior, not in putting me or anyone else under a glass to look for flaws. . . . I watched Bertha carefully. She aimed for perfection in her work and in her conduct, and was pleased when she hit the mark, but she had patience with herself when she missed, too. This was worth knowing, I thought. It's one thing to demand perfection or else, and quite another to hope for it and try for it."

*June Sprigg, describing her experience living with the six remaining Shaker sisters at Canterbury during the summer of 1972, in* Simple Gifts: A Memoir of a Shaker Village, *1998*

*Above left: Trinity Church, Cornish.* Photograph by Walker Evans, 1972. The simple blocky geometry of many a New Hampshire church expresses an unquestioning, solid faith. *Hood Museum of Art, Dartmouth College. Above right:* Bentwood shaker baskets and boxes were a commercial mainstay for the Canterbury community. *Canterbury Shaker Village. Photo Bill Finney*

This covered bridge near Stark is one of many in the state. The 460-foot span over the Connecticut River between Cornish, New Hampshire, and Windsor, Vermont, is the longest wooden covered bridge in the U.S. *Photo David Brownell*

## Making Tracks

Traveling through the White Mountains on foot has greatly improved over the centuries, and more than 5,000 miles of hiking trails now lace the 780,000-acre White Mountain National Forest, New England's largest tract of public land. The first trail to Mount Washington's summit was cut in 1820 by legendary mountain man Ethan Allen Crawford, whose family also ran the first tourist hotel. The Crawford Path is America's oldest recreational trail in continuous use. By the late 1870s, the hiking enthusiasts of the Appalachian Mountain Club (AMC) began cutting and maintaining trails up other peaks and between mountains. The nation's most climbed mountain, 3,166-foot Mount Monadnock, stands alone southwest of the Whites.

*Left: Summit of Mount Washington* by Catherine Tuttle, 1999. The summit of Mount Washington is the apex for hikers seeking membership in the 4,000-Footer Club by climbing all 48 New Hampshire peaks over 4,000 feet. *McGowan Fine Art. Below:* The Crawford House hotel specialized in trail rides to the summit of Mount Washington, using the bridle trail cut by Ethan Allen Crawford in the 1820s. *New Hampshire Historical Society*

EVERY MORN I LIFT MY HEAD,
See New England underspread
South from St. Lawrence to the Sound,
From Katskill east to the sea-bound.

*Ralph Waldo Emerson, from "Monadnoc," 1847*

Nineteenth-century quarry. *University of New Hampshire, courtesy Gary Samson*

## Block of Ages

Since late Colonial days, New Hampshire stonecutters have quarried white, pink, and gray granites from four major deposits. Tight-grained and uniform, New Hampshire granite makes an imperial building stone that's been used extensively in grand constructions such as the Library of Congress in Washington, D.C. But frugal Granite Staters often balked at the premium price of local stone, importing cheaper Maine or Vermont granite. A notable exception is the civic heart of Concord, the capital city, blessed with quarries less than three miles away. Builders of the New Hampshire State House employed local granite dressed up with Vermont marble. Finished in 1819, it is now the oldest state capitol where the legislature still meets in its original chambers. More typically, Granite State stone is used for memorials and embellishment: the white granite arch that dominates the broad plaza in front of the state house, and the pedestals there that support statues of New Hampshire historic figures. Close by, the massive sculpture above the entrance of the New Hampshire Historical Society building depicts the "progress of history"; native-born Daniel Chester French took more than six months to carve it from a single 22-ton block of Concord granite.

*Above:* **New Hampshire capitol building.** *Ralph Morang. Left:* **Daniel Chester French's** *Ancient and Modern History* **crowns the main entry to the New Hampshire Historical Society Library.** *New Hampshire Historical Society*

## Over the River, Through the Woods

New Hampshire's glacial topography of ridges and ditches running north-south posed a challenge to early travelers. Anyone who wanted to go east-west had to cross the hills and ford the waters. Small-town farmers excelled at building bridges—usually a planked roadway sheltered with a roof and braced on each side with a wooden truss.

Until proprietary designs emerged in the 1830s, most bridges employed the queen truss, handed down by generations of barn and church builders. In 1830, Colonel Stephen H. Long of Hopkinton patented his Long truss, said to be the first scientific truss design. The state still boasts more than four dozen covered bridges, including the 460-foot span over the Connecticut River between Cornish, New Hampshire, and Windsor, Vermont, the longest wooden covered bridge in the U.S.

Crossing the southern flank of the White Mountains was a steeper challenge. The first road, cleared and packed in 1837, went only halfway, following the valley of the Swift River. Not until 1937 did engineers venture to lay pavement across the 4,000-foot divide between Conway and the lumber town of Lincoln. The twisting two-lane road through the White Mountains National Forest opened to traffic in 1959 as the Kancamagus Highway—the finest foliage road in the National Forest system.

The 1869 Paddleford construction bridge over the Swift River in Conway is one of the longest in the White Mountains National Forest. *Photo S. R. Maglione/Photo Researchers*

Primary campaigning is a sure sign of late winter in a presidential election year. New Hampshire's primary elections have thrust many a candidate into the national spotlight. *Photo Owen Franken/Corbis*

## Presidential Primaries

Many a presidential candidacy has flourished or withered on the stony political soil of New Hampshire's first-in-the-nation primary elections. Print and broadcast media give Granite Staters a national forum for their views and concerns, as voters make the first division of sheep from goats in our quadrennial winter of discontent. Their accuracy is better than most oddsmakers': In the last 10 elections through 1996, New Hampshire primary victors won their party nominations six times (Democrats) and eight times (Republicans). The citizens of Dixville Notch step to the fore again in the fall general election, voting precisely at midnight and releasing the count moments later. Commentators can rarely read a trend, as Dixville Notch usually splits evenly between the major parties.

"IN PRIMARY SEASON CRYSTALBALLING IS A serious cottage industry: last time our phone rang seven times from out-of-state professional pollsters. There are two ways to win the primary in New Hampshire: one is to do better than opponents, the other is to do better than expectations."

*Ronald Jager, Last House on the Road: Excursions Into a Rural Past, 1994*

## The Granite State President

Often a kingmaker, only once did New Hampshire supply the king. In 1852 the deadlocked Democratic party convention turned to obscure New Hampshire lawyer Franklin Pierce on the 49th ballot. He trounced Whig candidate General Winfield Scott in the general election, but stumbled domestically by inflaming the slavery issue and internationally by secretly seeking to acquire Cuba from Spain. He is best remembered for appointing his Bowdoin College classmate (and biographer) Nathaniel Hawthorne to administrative and foreign policy posts. Pierce's childhood home in Hillsborough is a history museum.

When Isadore and Lucille Zimmerman moved into their boxy Frank Lloyd Wright Usonian house in Manchester in 1952, neighbors dismissed it as "that chicken coop." *Currier Gallery of Art, Manchester. Photo Sarbo/CGA*

## Building for the Ages

New Hampshire's first colonists settled at the mouth of the Piscataqua harbor, bringing with them the English town square and its small building lots. From the outset, domestic architecture made the most of limited land and plentiful lumber. Built in 1664, the Jackson House in Portsmouth is New Hampshire's oldest surviving house and among the earliest examples of plank frame construction in New England. Almost every style of New Hampshire dwelling—from saltbox to gambrel-roofed manse, from boxy farmhouse to narrow tenement—is found in Strawbery Banke Museum, a 10-acre site where

Portsmouth's preservationists countered the ravages of mid-20th century urban renewal. Some structures have stood for two or even three centuries.

A desire "to be done forever with living in the 18th century," however, prompted Isadore and Lucille Zimmerman of Manchester to commission one of Frank Lloyd Wright's Usonian homes, based on his principles of elegant and affordable housing. When the Zimmermans moved into their low-rise, boxy house in 1952, neighbors dismissed it as "that chicken coop." Better appreciated now, the revolutionary home is owned by the Currier Gallery of Art and is the only Wright house open to the public in New England.

The Warner House murals in Portsmouth, restored in 1988, date from close to the home's construction in 1719. Drawn from European prints, they represent some of the earliest colonial murals still in place. *Photo Ralph Morang*

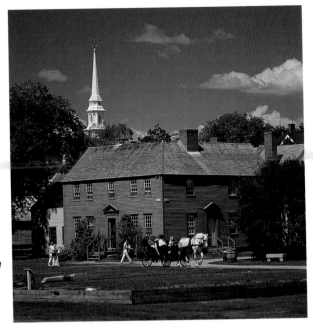

## Portsmouth Privilege

By the mid-18th century, Portsmouth had captured most of
New Hampshire wealth by controlling the mast trade in tall
pines and the sea trade in all manner of goods. Its merchant
princes employed shipbuilding artisans to construct homes on
a scale grand enough to rival Newburyport, Salem, and
Boston, Massachusetts.

Organizations such as the Society of Colonial Dames and
the Society for the Preservation of New England Antiquities

eventually acquired several of the grandest, including six downtown mansions that now operate as house-museums, preserving the magisterial architecture and the personalities of their creators. The gardens of the Moffat-Ladd House, for example, still contain English damask roses grown from the 1763 bridal bouquet of the first inhabitant; each new generation takes clippings at wedding time. A more modest manse is named for John Paul Jones, one of the boarders taken in by a widow whose husband (and fortune) went down with his ship. With his privateer's fortune, John Langdon built a Georgian

manor house with carved woodwork and a grand dining room. When George Washington visited in 1789, he was duly impressed, to Langdon's delight. The newest of the group, the Rundlet-May House, was gadgeteer James Rundlet's showpiece of state-of-the-art technology in 1807.

"[IN PORTSMOUTH] MERCHANT princes were able to build themselves wooden palaces with white walls and green shutters, of a grandeur and beauty unmatched elsewhere in the country."

*William Dean Howells,*
Literature and Life, *1902*

## Fine Things for Fine Houses

Granite State furniture makers were noted for their idiosyncratic styles. The Dunlap dynasty of cabinetmakers in the Merrimack Valley began with Major John Dunlap (1746–92) of Bedford, a farmer known for his high chests characterized by a galleried pediment with shells and pierced fretwork.

Dunlap generally completed his furniture by March, freeing himself for spring planting. His brother and their sons continued the business through the 19th century. Several makers of distinctive furniture served Portsmouth's wealthy clientele, beginning with John Gaines III (1704–43), remembered chiefly for his intricately carved chairs. By the early Federal period, Portsmouth cabinetmakers developed a flamboyant regional style employing contrasting colors, blaze-figured veneers, fine inlays, and geometric patterns of panels, doors, and drawers. Among the most successful were the joiner-cabinetmakers Jonathan Judkins and William Senter, both active in the early 19th century.

Chest on chest frame, Hennicker or Salisbury, 1790–95. The Dunlap family dynasty of furniture makers developed a style found widely in the Merrimack Valley. This maple and pine chest may have been fashioned by Lieutenant Samuel Dunlap (1752–1830). *Currier Gallery of Art, Manchester*

## Great Gardeners

Granite Staters love their flowers—the wash of wild roses at the sea's edge or the farmhouse dooryard succession of lilacs, daylilies, and chrysanthemums. Rose Nichols and Celia Thaxter raised flower gardening in New Hampshire to an art, and while most gardens pass with their makers, the plantings they described so vividly in their own words have been re-created. Sometimes called America's first female landscape architect, Nichols traveled in Europe and wrote extensively on the design of formal gardens. Beginning in 1889, she spent summers in Cornish, initially to be near her beloved "Uncle Gus"—sculptor Augustus Saint-Gaudens. At Mastlands, the family summer home, Nichols put her observations to the test with formal gardens that delighted the Cornish colony.

More than 500 varieties of annuals are planted each year in Prescott Park in Portsmouth as part of the All-American selections trials. *Photo Nance S. Trueworthy/Stock Boston*

**Celia Thaxter's garden on Appledore Island has been restored to the design that so delighted her guests in the 1890s.**
*Photo Ralph Morang/New England Stock Photo*

Portsmouth-born poet and essayist Celia Thaxter created effusive flower gardens at her family's resort hotel on Appledore Island in the Isles of Shoals (technically a few hundred feet over the state line in Maine). Her plantings inspired many famous guests among the Boston literati, and at the end of her life, in 1894, she published the now-classic *An Island Garden.* The watercolor illustrations by her friend and frequent hotel guest Childe Hassam rank among the high-water marks of American Impressionism.

*In the Garden* by Childe Hassam, 1892. Childe Hassam was a frequent visitor to the Thaxter family hotel on Appledore Island, just over the Maine boundary line in the Isles of Shoals. He illustrated Celia Thaxter's classic gardening book, *An Island Garden*, reserving this portrait of the author for the frontispiece. *National Museum of American Art/Art Resource, NY*

"I LOVE TO PORE OVER EVERY BLOSSOM THAT UNFOLDS IN THE GARDEN, no matter what it may be, to study it and learn it by heart as far as a poor mortal may. If one but gazes closely into a tiny flower of the pale blue Forget-me-not, what a chapter of loveliness is there!"

*Celia Thaxter,* An Island Garden, *1894*

A sport born of using draft animals to haul logs and ice from the woods, horse-pulling contests are still a mainstay of New Hampshire fairs and holiday festivities. Fair season starts just after the first haying in July and concludes after the October apple harvest. Rochester and Deerfield host the oldest fairs, running since 1875 and 1876. Each draws around 150,000 people. *Photo David Brownell*

## Simple Pleasures

With its sparse roads and scattered farms, 19th-century rural New Hampshire created excuses for people to go to town. Asphalt has replaced gravel and subdivisions have carved up cow pastures, but bucolic community gatherings persist. On Saturday nights in July and August for the last four decades, locals and tourists alike have flocked to the United Methodist Church on Main Street in Moultonborough for "Famous Baked Bean Suppers": two kinds of beans, hot dogs, potato salad, homemade brown bread, and pies. Every Wednesday between Independence and Labor Days, hundreds gather at dusk in Wolfeboro's Cate Park to hear the town band play. Many a town-hall closet is filled with instruments, and almost every town green has a bandstand. Temple's town band is said to be the nation's oldest.

"A BAND CONCERT WAS AN OCCASION, AND I NEVER HAD any trouble persuading Father to let me hitch up the fringe-top surrey. As seven o'clock drew near, farm families arrived from miles around. The village folks brought out chairs, and an audience of three hundred or more made themselves comfortable around the common. The tall white church spire loomed overhead; the village school was across the common; the red brick vestry was across the street from the white circular bandstand with its green shingled roof. There was a hush as Mr. Peavey lifted his baton, waited for a dramatic second, and then brought it down as the band struck up a stirring march."

*Haydn S. Pearson*, New England Flavor: Memories of a Country Boyhood, *1961*

## Fresh Refrigerator Pickles

3 large cucumbers
1 green bell pepper
1 onion
1 tbsp. salt
2 tsp. celery seeds
¼ cup sugar
½ cup white vinegar

Scrub unpeeled cucumbers and cut into ⅛-in. slices. Finely chop bell pepper and onion; combine with cucumbers in a large bowl. Sprinkle with salt and celery seeds, mix well and let stand at least 1 hour. Dissolve sugar in vinegar and pour over the vegetables, stirring to blend. Cover and refrigerate at least 1 day before serving.

*From* A Hancock Community Collection, First Congregational Church, Hancock

Almost every New Hampshire town has a bandstand on its town green. Few town bands still exist, but the stages get a good workout from visiting performers. The Metropolitan Brass Quartet serenades the crowd at New London near Lake Sunapee.
*Photo David Brownell*

## Rev It Up

New Hampshire is fascinated by motorized speed. As long ago as 1869, Sylvester H. Roper of Francestown hooked a small steam engine to a clunky velocipede and puffed around town. He refined his invention to work with the smaller bicycle and smoked New England's top cyclists in an 1896 demonstration in Boston. Alas, Roper did not get to savor his triumph. The 73-year-old inventor died in the saddle from a heart attack at 40 mph. Virgil D. White of West Ossipee mounted skis on the front and rotary treads on the back of an old Ford chassis, and dubbed his device the "snowmobile." White's Snowmobile Company factory cranked out 3,500 machines a year between

The New Hampshire International Speedway inaugurated Indy car racing in July 1992.
*Photo Dean Abramson/ Stock Boston*

1920 and 1928. Originally used to carry mail and transport doctors in the winter backcountry, snowmobiles became so popular for sport that New Hampshire clubs now maintain more than 6,000 miles of groomed trails.

Granite State hillsides echo with the sound of open throttles in mid-June, when 150,000 motorcyclists descend on Laconia and Weirs Beach for the annual Motorcycle Week. Held since 1939, the gathering of the clubs gained national notoriety for the 1965 riots chronicled in Hunter S. Thompson's *Hell's Angels.* The highlight of the week is the AMA Loudon Classic track race, America's oldest motorcycle competition.

*Above:* When snow blankets the landscape, even some police officers take to snowmobiles to get around. Since the practical vehicle was invented in New Hampshire, snowmobiling has become a leading form of winter recreation. *Photo L. O'Shaughnessy/New England Stock Photo. Left:* Vintage class 1953 Allard participates in the Mount Washington Auto Hill climb. *Photo William Johnson/Stock Boston*

The MacDowell Colony's aim has always been to provide seclusion for artists to work in peace. *New Hampshire Historical Society*

### The MacDowell Colony

American composer Edward MacDowell reckoned that the tranquility of his log-cabin summer retreat in Peterborough, New Hampshire, trebled his creative output. As a founder of the American Academy in Rome, he also believed that artists from different disciplines stimulated each other creatively. Faced with failing health, MacDowell dreamed of transforming his Peterborough farm into a community where artists could work in solitude by day and interact with each other by night. Influential friends assembled a fund in his name and in 1907 the MacDowell Colony was born. More than 4,500 composers, writers, visual artists, filmmakers, interdisciplinary artists, and architects have retreated to MacDowell over the years, producing work as colloquial as Thornton Wilder's *Our Town,* as groundbreaking as Aaron Copland's *Appalachian Spring,* and as timeless as Leonard Bernstein's *Mass.* More than 200 artists annually pass through the MacDowell community, electing to commune with their work in the New Hampshire woods.

James Baldwin. *Chester Higgins, Jr./Photo Researchers*

"I WILL BE VERY GLAD . . . TO BE WORKING AT the Colony—which for many years now has lived in my mind as a refuge and a workshop and the place in which I most wanted to be when the time comes, as it perpetually does, to crouch in order to spring."

*Novelist James Baldwin,
in a MacDowell Colony statement*

"ON VARIOUS OCCASIONS IN THAT SPARTAN PARADISE MY SANITY HAS been restored. When I am there my very best work is composed, when I am far away, the fact of the place allows me to breathe more easily."

*Composer Ned Rorem, in a MacDowell Colony statement*

**W**hen the late Robb Sagendorph launched *Yankee* magazine in Dublin in 1935, he announced in typically laconic fashion that its mission was "the expression, and perhaps indirectly, the preservation of our New England culture." Over the years it has become a standard-bearer of Yankee character in an often untraditional New England world. From the problem-solving of Earl Proulx (how to flatten a warped plank) to the "Swopper's Column" ("Will swop Christmas ornaments and collectible Santa for Nancy Drew board game"), *Yankee* upholds the image of New England frugality, if not folksiness. Says editor Judson Hale, "I would rather *Yankee* crawl away into a forest and die than actually be *folksy.*"

In a single issue, the magazine might report on a priest who specializes in rebuilding rundown parish churches or the rare seabirds of Maine's north coast. Even the dark side of New England life creeps into its pages, such as a cautionary tale about a lottery player caught in a deadly spiral of post-winning excesses. While panegyrics about wildlife and scenery are part of *Yankee's* stock in trade, the magazine's editorial forte has been and remains tales of people. ❄

Over the years, *Yankee* magazine has come to speak for the region of New England. *Photo Doug Mindell*

"AROUND HERE IT'S BEST TO START AS YOUNG AS POSSIBLE ON THE main business of life. . . . Pretty much living by your wits, fleecing the summer people, marrying smart women, doing about everything that comes to hand but avoiding really hard work, and of course, keeping the town taxes down."

*Robb Sagendorph, deadpanning a slick* Life *magazine reporter with his description of Yankee lifestyle, in Judson Hale's autobiography,* The Education of a Yankee, *1987*

**Yankee Publishing's headquarters in Dublin, right next to the community church, are in keeping with the magazine's unswerving support for a rural New England lifestyle.** *Photo Jim Schwabel/New England Stock*

**Robert Frost.** *Gary Samson, University of New Hampshire*

**T**he authentic literature of New Hampshire has the unflinching quality of tough plants that thrive in rocky soil. Visiting 19th-century writers spied the sublime in the state's alpine scenery, but its modern writers have looked on the mountains and seen their hard, cold stone. One lone figure, Robert Frost, rescued New Hampshire from transcendental pieties, resetting the course of New England literature with the publication in 1913 of *A Boy's Will* and in 1915 of *North of Boston.* Although the one-time Derry chicken farmer and schoolteacher moved in and out of the state, his first six books were written in New Hampshire. He won his first of four Pulitzer prizes in 1924 for the book-length poem *New Hampshire.* In a 1937 letter to the editors of the WPA guide to New Hampshire, Frost recounted his intimate relationship with Derry and Franconia and general kinship with the state, concluding, "So you see, it has been New Hampshire, New Hampshire with me all the way. You will find my poems show it, I think." ❄

"THE FIGURE A POEM MAKES. IT BEGINS IN DELIGHT
and ends in wisdom. The figure is the same as for love."

*Robert Frost, in the preface to his* Collected Poems, *1939*

**Robert Frost's farm in Franconia.** *Porterfield/Chickering/Photo Researchers*

SOMETHING THERE IS THAT DOESN'T LOVE A WALL,
That sends the frozen ground-swell under it,
And spills the upper boulders in the sun;
And makes gaps even two can pass abreast.
. . .
I let my neighbor know beyond the hill;
And on a day we meet to walk the line
And set the wall between us once again.
We keep the wall between us as we go. . . .

*From "Mending Wall" by Robert Frost, in* North of Boston, *1914*

## The Flowering After Frost

Frost's absence from the Granite State was ameliorated by the presence of Richard Eberhart, who served as Dartmouth's poet-in-residence from 1956–84. The flowering after Frost continued with poets as reflective as Jane Kenyon and as observant of the sheer lusciousness of experience as Mekeel McBride. Charles Simic, with his gnomic intellect, and Maxine Kumin, who often locates internal conflicts in a pastoral landscape, share little except their state of residence, their mastery of expression, and their Pulitzer laurels.

Since relocating in 1975 to the New Hampshire of his boyhood, essayist and poet Donald Hall has been America's correspondent from Frost country. His ruminations on life at Eagle Pond and environs have made him the definitive chronicler of changing rural life. The state's poet laureate, Hall writes a precise verse that inscribes human dilemmas upon a bleak land-

Many novels by New Hampshire native John Irving have been made into films, including *The Hotel New Hampshire*. Photofest

scape. Novelist John Irving is one of New Hampshire's few native writers, drawing on the prep school life of his Exeter boyhood as background for many of his early novels. Ironically, the most famous writer in the state, the reclusive J. D. Salinger, has not published since moving to Cornish three decades ago.

MAKING WAY FOR ONE RADISH MIGHT MEAN
shovelling up stones the size
of sewing baskets; for cabbage,
dislodging rock that weighed more
than our woodstove; and in exchange
for tomatoes, a boulder bigger than a sofa.

*Mekeel McBride, from "Growing Stones in New Hampshire"*
*in* Red Letter Days, *1988*

Poet and essayist Donald Hall of Wilmot has become New Hampshire's leading literary voice. *Photo Ralph Morang*

"I LIVE IN THE HOUSE I ALWAYS WANTED TO LIVE IN. WHEN I WAS A boy, spending summers here with my grandmother and grandfather, I wrote poems and read books in the morning; in the afternoon I hayed with my grandfather, listening to his long, slow stories of old times. I loved him, and he gave me the past of his boyhood as if it were a fortune or a mild chronic disease."

*Donald Hall,* Here at Eagle Pond, *1990*

The New London Barn Playhouse in the Lake Sunapee region is one of the Granite State's very active summer theaters. Others include the Lakes Region Summer Theater in Meredith (Lake Winnipesaukee) and the Mount Washington Valley Theatre Company in North Conway. *Photo David Brownell*

### Summer Song and Dance

"*Our Town* is an attempt to find value above all price for the events in our daily life," wrote Thornton Wilder. In his 1938 Pulitzer prize—winning play, Peterborough is thinly disguised as Grover's Corners, a town where simple pleasures take the place of high culture. Yet summer brings theater and music to New Hampshire to augment those simple joys. The Barnstormers, once directed by the son of President Grover Cleveland, present a full season of old chestnuts and new amusements in their wood-frame theater in the Winnipesaukee-area village of Tamworth, while the Peterborough Players, founded in 1933, produce quintessential summer theater in an 18th-century barn. Midcentury touring stock companies have been superseded by local producers of musical comedy and similar light fare in vacation spots.

## Sweet Pastorales

Classical and chamber music echo across the green fields during July and August, with the Apple Hill Chamber Players of Nelson and the North Country Chamber Players of Lincoln presenting monthlong series of concerts. The New Hampshire Music Festival in Gilford is the state's premier classical music series, while the Lake Winnipesaukee Music Festival in Wolfeboro combines a chamber music series with extensive educational programs for young musicians. Peterborough's Monadnock Music Summer Festival has the broadest scope of all, encompassing chamber music, piano recitals, orchestral concerts, and operatic productions.

The Lake Winnipesaukee Chamber Players perform a summer concert. *Craig Alnee. Below:* Thornton Wilder's *Our Town,* based in large part on Peterborough, was an instant classic and won the playwright a Pulitzer prize. Wilder wrote much of the play while in residence at the MacDowell Colony. *Photofest*

". . . THERE ISN'T MUCH CULTURE; BUT MAYBE this is the place to tell you that we've got a lot of pleasures of a kind here: we like the sun comin' up over the mountain in the morning, and we all notice a good deal about the birds. We pay a lot of attention to them. And we watch the change of seasons; yes, everybody knows about them."

*Mr. Webb, publisher and editor of the Grover's Corners Sentinel, in Thornton Wilder's Our Town, 1938*

**B**rought to New York from Ireland by his French shoemaker father and Irish mother at the height of the potato famine in 1848, high-school dropout Augustus Saint-Gaudens studied art at the Cooper Union night school, apprenticed as a cameo cutter, and scrimped to book passage to Paris to study sculpture at the École des Beaux-Arts. When his monumental Central Park statue of Admiral Farragut was unveiled in 1878, his career was made. By 1885, Saint-Gaudens was planning his *Standing Lincoln* and seeking a summer retreat from Manhattan. Lawyer friend Charles Beaman suggested Cornish:

Augustus Saint-Gaudens sculpted at his Cornish estate during summers starting in 1885, and lived there year round in 1900 until his death in 1907. *Right:* $10 gold piece designed by Saint-Gaudens, first minted in 1907. *Both, Saint-Gaudens National Historic Site, Cornish*

"You will find plenty of Lincoln-shaped men up there for models." Saint-Gaudens transformed a chunky farmhouse into an estate with studios, formal gardens, and nature trails where he could sit under the pergola, ponder Mount Ascutney across the river, and dream neoclassical sculptures that defined an American imperial style. For 15 years he worked on commissions at "Aspet" in the summers, moving to Cornish full-time in 1900 until his death in 1907. Although known primarily for his heroic-scale public sculptures—*The Puritan* in Springfield, Massachusetts, the Shaw Memorial in Boston—at the end of his life he returned to small-scale bas-relief at the request of an old friend, Theodore Roosevelt, designing perhaps the most beautiful coins ever struck by the U.S. Mint: the $10 and $20 gold pieces known colloquially as the "eagle" and "double eagle." ❄

*Above, top:* **The 1897 Shaw Memorial by Saint-Gaudens, on the Boston Common in Massachusetts, commemorates black Civil War soldiers.**
*Above, bottom: Amor Caritas by Saint-Gaudens. Both, Saint-Gaudens National Historic Site, Cornish*

*Male Wood Duck in a Forest Pool (study for Concealing-Coloration in the Animal Kingdom)* by Abbott Thayer, 1905–1909. Principally a Beaux-Arts painter of mythological scenes and angels, Thayer made pioneering studies in camouflage and helped the U.S. armed forces develop camouflage clothing in World War I. *National Museum of American Art/Art Resource, N.Y.*

## The Cornish Colony

By the mid-1890s, a substantial coterie of New York, Boston, and Chicago artists and intellectuals had coalesced around Saint-Gaudens in what came to be called the Cornish Colony. Among them were such unlikely figures as the painter of Native Americans George de Forest Brush, who lived at first in a tepee erected on Saint-Gaudens's lawn, and chronicler of the American West Frederic Remington. Philadelphia painter Stephen Parrish coaxed his successful illustrator son, Maxfield, to build a house in nearby Plainfield in 1898, where the younger Parrish lived and worked year round until his death in 1966, often using his neighbors as models. While many painters came for the summer lushness of the Connecticut River Valley, Impressionist Willard Metcalf favored winter, creating some of his most delicate, Monet-like landscape paintings of icebound brooks and snowfield meadows.

"IT'S A LONG WAY FROM ROME TO CORNISH, New Hampshire. Yet it may give New Englanders a thrill to see on the banks of the Connecticut River, set in beauty and dignity, the evidences of a famous journey in art begun in the Eternal City and ending among the meadows of white pines and sheep pastures of the land we know so well."

*Homer Saint-Gaudens, writing of his father's estate in the Christian Science Monitor, 1922*

*Hunt Farm (Daybreak)* by Maxfield Parrish, 1948. Joining the Cornish Colony in 1898, Philadelphia-born Parrish outlasted all of his friends, living and painting in the region until his death in 1966. *Hood Museum of Art, Dartmouth College. ©Maxfield Parrish Family Trust/Licensed by ASaP, Holderness, N.H., and VAGA, N.Y.*

New Hampshire's White Mountains were a logical subject as American painters began to develop an indigenous approach to monumental landscape in the early 19th century. Thomas Cole, a founder of the Hudson River School, recorded the grandeur of the Whites on several canvases following an 1828 visit. Convinced of the pictorial possibilities of these mountains, New Ipswich–born painter Benjamin Champney founded an art colony in North Conway in the 1850s. He recorded in his autobiography that so many landscape painters were in residence "in 1853 and 1854 the meadows and banks of the Saco were dotted all about with white umbrellas." Among those who joined Champney in celebrating New Hampshire's peaks were Albert Bierstadt,

soon to gain widespread fame for spectacular paintings of the Rocky Mountains, and George Inness, whose style made the long march from Hudson River bombast to Impressionist intimation. As American landscape style evolved from the sublime to the subtle, the White Mountain School painters

*A View of the Mountain Pass Called the Notch of the White Mountains* by Thomas Cole, 1839. Cole's dramatic paintings of the White Mountains were instrumental in attracting other painters to depict the "sublime" landscapes. *National Gallery of Art, Washington, D.C.*

increasingly chose the flower-dotted rolling meadows of the Pemigewasset River Valley on the far side of the Presidential Range from their original North Conway base. ❄

New Hampshire was the first state to honor and support professional artisanry in traditional craft media. In 1932 the state government helped found the League of New Hampshire Arts & Crafts to encourage the preservation of such skills as hand-weaving, basket making, pottery, vegetable-dyeing, and wood carving. The league established workshops and adult education programs with master artists to enlarge the community of practitioners and create a sophisticated and receptive buying public. In 1933, the league held its first crafts fair, with proceeds reaching an unexpected $2,698. The annual fair—the oldest in the nation—remains one of the country's top juried showcases of artisanry.

This supportive environment made New Hampshire a mecca for

*Bird Clock* by Nancy Frost Begin, n.d. New Hampshire craftspeople often transform traditional craft products with contemporary decorative design. *Courtesy the artist. Photo Charley Frieberg, League of New Hampshire Craftsmen*

Duck decoy. *Photo Gary Samson*

crafts artists over the decades and a center of the studio crafts movement that blossomed in the late 1960s. To reflect a revised focus on crafts professionals, the league changed its name to the League of New Hampshire Craftsmen in 1968, and today has more than 900 juried members. In 1999, clay artist Gerry Williams, founder of *Studio Potter* magazine, was named New Hampshire's first Artist Laureate. ✳

*Above:* **Dan Dustin demonstrates traditional spoon carving at the annual fair of the League of New Hampshire Craftsmen.** *Photo Charley Frieberg, League of New Hampshire Craftsmen.* *Left:* **Traditional oak splint basketry.** *Photo Gary Samson*

With its relatively low cost of living and proximity to the Boston metropolis, New Hampshire has become a haven for emerging artists as well as a summer and year-round retreat for established figures such as filmmaker Ken Burns. The studio art program and gallery at the University of New Hampshire in Durham acts as a magnet on the seacoast, while the New Hampshire Institute of Art in Manchester—the state's only independent art college—is a locus of activity in the Merrimack Valley, offering classes and an exhibition gallery.

*Ram-Headed Men* by Dan Dailey, 1998. Ranked among the world's leading glass artists, Dailey combines the formality of glass with a postmodern comic sensibility. *Courtesy the artist. Photo Bill Truslow. Right: Icon for the Musical Ratios of Nature* by Carol Aronson-Shore. *Bank of New Hampshire; McGowan Fine Art*

The Hood Museum of Art at Dartmouth College features northern New England artists, many from New Hampshire, in a biennial spotlight exhibition. The Art Center in Hargate at St. Paul's School in Concord operates a gallery program featuring regional and national

artists. The Franco-American Center in Manchester specializes in work by the descendants of the Merrimack Valley's French-speaking immigrants, who brought strong woodcarving and musical traditions with them from Quebec.

Professional associations play a substantial role in the state's artistic life. Members of the New Hampshire Art Association, hewing to the traditions of Granite State art, tend to favor landscapes and seascapes, and the association's Portsmouth gallery operates a busy exhibition program of members' work. ❋

*Above: Hawthorn Twig by John Hatch, 1950 Left: Untitled by Erick Hufschmid, 1988. Courtesy the artist*

### Astronomy that Rocks

Aptly named Mystery Hill in North Salem is the site of America's Stonehenge, a series of stone walls where shaped standing stones function as an astronomical calendar, and multi-ton capstones cover underground chambers. Radio-carbon dating suggests the site could be 4,000 years old, making it the only megalithic construction in North America.

### Writing on the Walls

The murals on the reading-room walls of Dartmouth College's Baker Library are entitled *Epic of American Civilization.* The 3,000 square feet of paintings caused quite a stir when Mexican muralist José Clemente Orozco finished them in 1934. Now restored, the murals illustrate events in American culture—before and after contact with Europeans—in a vigorous Expressionist style.

### Overarching Praise

Named for rich benefactor Charles Tilton, the Tilton Arch is an exact replica of the Arch of Titus in Rome. Executed in Concord granite, the 55-foot arch is capped with a recumbent red granite lion. Situated in adjoining Northfield, the arch overlooks the town of Tilton, which is dotted with monuments commissioned by Charles Tilton for the "betterment" of the populace.

## Main Street: High and Wide

Keene claims that its Main Street is the widest in the world, thanks to the first settlers who gave up property to create the broad thoroughfare that served as an open marketplace. That market mentality helped Keene reverse the trend of retailers jumping ship for the malls: Main Street, Keene, is where southwest New Hampshire shops.

## High-Caliber Cooperage

The largest wooden barrel in the world, according to the Guinness Book of World Records, is displayed at the Red Hook Ale Brewery in Portsmouth. Measuring 16 feet high and 10 feet wide, the barrel was constructed in 1998 by the Spaulding & Frost Cooperage of Fremont, the oldest pine cooperage still in operation.

## Slippery Slope

The New England Ski Museum at Franconia Notch chronicles more than a century of downhill sport with artifacts that range from planklike early skis and bamboo poles to the high-tech marvels on the slopes today. One display even shows the metal pins used to stabilize broken bones.

## Great People

*A selective listing of native Granite Staters, concentrating on the arts.*

**Daniel Chester French**
(1850–1931), sculptor

**Thomas Bailey Aldrich**
(1836–1907), author and editor of
the *Atlantic Monthly*

**Amy Beach** (1867–1944), composer

**George Bissell** (1821–1884), oil
well–drilling pioneer

**Charles Farrar Browne** ("Arte-
mus Ward") (1834–67), journalist
and humorist

**Salmon Portland Chase**
(1808–1873), Chief Justice of the
Supreme Court and co-founder
of the Republican Party

**Barbara Ann Cochran** (b. 1951),
Olympic gold medal skier

**Ralph Adams Cram** (1863–1942),
architect and leading exponent
of the Gothic Revival style

**Charles Dana** (1819–1897), journalist and editor

**Mary Baker Eddy** (1821–1910),
founder of the Church of Christ,
Scientist

**Barry Faulkner** (1881–1966),
painter known for murals at
National Archives and Rockefeller Center

**Carlton Fisk** (b. 1947), Baseball
Hall of Fame catcher

**Joseph F. Glidden** (1813–1906),
inventor; first to manufacture
practical barbed-wire fencing

**Horace Greeley** (1811–1872), journalist and founder of the *New
York Tribune*

**Sarah Josepha Hale** (1788–1879),
social reformer, novelist, editor
of *Godey's Lady's Book,* and author
of the children's poem "Mary
had a little lamb"

**George W. Kendall** (1809–1867),

founder of the *New Orleans
Picayune*

**Walter Kittredge** (1836–1905),
songwriter, best known for
"Tenting on the Old Camp
Ground"

**William Ladd** (1778–1841), pacifist
nicknamed the "Apostle of
Peace"

**William Loeb** (1905–1991), presi-
dent and publisher of *Manchester
Union–Leader* and *New Hampshire
Sunday News*

**Joyce Maynard** (b. 1953), essayist, memoirist, novelist

**Grace Metalious** (1924–1964),
author of *Peyton Place*

**Henry P. Moore** (1835–1911), lith-
ographer of N.H. scenes and
Civil War photographer

**Charles A. Pillsbury** (1842–1899),
founder of C. A. Pillsbury & Co.,
which became the largest flour
miller in the world

**David Souter** (b. 1939), U.S.
Supreme Court Justice

**John Stark** (1728–1822), Revolutionary War general

# . . . and Great Places

*Some interesting derivations of New Hampshire place names.*

**Agassiz Basin**   Rock formation named for naturalist Louis Agassiz, who visited in 1847 and 1870.

**Ballou City**   Lore holds that the name was bestowed by a visitor skeptical of tall tales told in the tavern about a local man's reputed conjuring powers.

**Bennington**   Named for colonial governor Benning Wentworth.

**Fabyan**   Named for early hotel pioneer Horace Fabyan.

**Gilsum**   The name was a compromise to honor both town founders, Gilbert and Summer.

**Hanover**   Named for the reigning house of Great Britain at the time of the 1765 settlement.

**Isles of Shoals**   Named for the "shoaling" or "schooling" of fish around the group of islands.

**Kinsman Notch**   Named for pioneer Asa Kinsman, who used an axe to cut his way through the notch, refusing to turn back when he found he was on the wrong road.

**Lake Umbagog**   From Algonquian term for "muddy water."

**Manchester**   In emulation of the English manufacturing city, the town's name was changed from Derryfield to Manchester in 1810.

**Monadnock**   From the Algonquian phrase "place of the surpassing mountain"; came to represent all large chunks of erosion-resistant rock left standing above a glacial plain.

**Mount Cabot**   For navigator Sebastian Cabot, son of the English discoverer of North America, John Cabot.

**Piscataqua River**   From Algonquian term for "dividing point of waters."

**Redstone**   Named for the red granite found in the area.

**Samoset Island**   Lore has it that this Winnipesaukee island was named for the only red-headed Native American ever known in the area.

**Smuttynose**   Sailors' name for island with long black point of rock jutting out into the sea.

**Stark**   Named for Revolutionary War general John Stark.

**Whittier**   Named for 19th-century poet John Greenleaf Whittier, who summered here.

**Wolfeborough**   Honors British general James Wolfe, who led the attack on Quebec City and was fatally wounded on the Plains of Abraham.

**Lake Sunapee**   From Algonquian term for "wild goose water."

# NEW HAMPSHIRE BY THE SEASONS
## A Perennial Calendar of Events and Festivals

*Here is a selective listing of events that take place each year in the months noted;*
*we suggest calling ahead to local chambers of commerce for dates and details.*

## January

Bartlett/Lower Bartlett
*BankBoston Celebrity Ski Classic*
Fundraiser supports children
with genetic and birth defects.

## March

Bartlett/Lower Bartlett
*Ski for the Cure*
Benefit race raises money for
New England Cystic Fibrosis
Foundation.

## March/April

Lincoln
*Easter Egg Hunt*
Children search for more than
4,000 eggs.

## April

Durham
*Faculty Concert Series*
Creative Arts Center faculty
present free concerts all month.

## May

Bethlehem
*Quilt Show and Sale*
Features work by North
Country quiltmakers.

Lisbon
*Lilac-Time Festival*
Parade, flea market, carnival,
and fireworks.

Loudon
*New Hampshire International
Speedway Races*
Opening day at the raceway fea-
tures the NASCAR Busch
Grand National 200.

New Boston
*Sheep & Wool Festival*
Celebration of country traditions includes sheepdog
demonstrations, workshops,
auction, crafts booths.

Portsmouth
*Heritage Plant Sale*
Sale of antique plant varieties at
Strawbery Banke Museum.

*Chowder Festival*
Some 20 restaurants serve 500-
plus gallons of chowder.

Winnipesaukee
*Winni Derby*
Landlocked salmon and
lake trout derby on Lake
Winnipesaukee.

## June

Canterbury
*Herb Day*
Sales of herbs and perennials
and garden tours at Canterbury
Shaker Village.

Gorham
*Climb to the Clouds*

Mt. Washington Auto Road Hill
Race to the summit is nation's
oldest motor-sports event.

Keene
*Monadnock Valley Indian Festival
& Pow Wow*
Dancing, singing, and vendors.

Laconia
*Motorcycle Rally and Race Week*
Since 1939 the hills have roared
with motorcycle races, hill
climbs, touring, and parades.

Milford
*Joseph Campbell Festival of Myth,
Folklore & Story*
Features music, puppetry,
storytelling, and dance.

Nashua
*New Hampshire Rose Society
Rose Show*
Competitive display by growers
from all over New England.

Pinkham Notch
*Mount Washington Road Race*
Footrace to the summit attracts
elite runners and amateurs.

## July

Bretton Woods
*Native American Cultural
Weekend*
Gathering of Native American
peoples.

Exeter
*Revolutionary War Festival*
Battle reenactments, 18th-century military encampment.

New London
*New London Garden Club Antiques Show*
Popular event features flower arrangements and plant sale.

Pembroke
*Antique Fire Apparatus Show and Meet*
Classic fire vehicles take part in parade, displays, and pumping demonstrations.

Portsmouth
*Bow Street Fair*
City's oldest crafts festival features more than 100 artisans.

Weirs Beach
*Antique and Classic Boat Show*
Juried show features more than 100 antique and modern boats.

Wolfeboro
*Lakes Region Open Waterski Tournament*
Competition for all ages features slalom and jumping.

## August

Bartlett/Lower Bartlett
*Equine Festival*
International show jumpers compete at Attitash Bear Park.

Campton
*Pemi Valley Bluegrass Festival*
Features acoustic bluegrass and old-time country bands of regional and national stature.

Canterbury
*Mother Ann Day*
Shaker holiday commemorates Shaker founder Ann Lee.

Lincoln
*Professional Lumberjack Festival*
Celebrates woodsmen's skills such as axe throwing, tree climbing, and birling.

Manchester
*New Hampshire Antique Dealers Association Annual Show*
Top-quality show caps New Hampshire's statewide Antiques Week.

Newbury
*League of New Hampshire Craftsmen Fair*
Juried show sets high standard; the oldest in the nation, held for more than 60 years.

Portsmouth
*Blues Festival*
New England's oldest annual blues festival.

## September

Deerfield
*Deerfield Fair*
World champion horse-pulling contest highlights oldest agricultural fair in N.H.

Portsmouth
*Grand Old Portsmouth Brewers Festival*
At Strawbery Banke Museum; highlights New England microbreweries.

Rochester
*Rochester Fair*
Harness racing at one of state's oldest agricultural fairs.

## October

Barrington
*Fall Foliage Festival*
Hayrides, pie-eating contest, produce displays, and auction.

Gilford
*Octoberfest*
Music, folk dance, and German food booths; at Gunstock Recreation Area.

Keene
*Pumpkin Festival*
Main Street is lined with glowing pumpkins. In 1998 it set a Guinness World Record: 17,693 jack-o'-lanterns in a single place.

Laconia
*Quilt Show*
Event at Belknap Mill features quilt display booths.

## November

Dover
*Holiday Parade*
Thanksgiving weekend parade through historic downtown: bands, antique vehicles.

## December

Portsmouth
*Candlelight Stroll*
Walk through Strawbery Banke Museum emphasizes winter activities and decorations.

# WHERE TO GO
## Museums, Attractions, Gardens, and Other Arts Resources

*Call for seasons and hours when open.*

## Museums

CANTERBURY SHAKER VILLAGE
288 Shaker Rd., Canterbury, 603-783-9511
*National Historic Landmark site has 25 original Shaker buildings, nature trails, and gardens on 694 acres.*

CORNISH COLONY GALLERY & MUSEUM
Rte. 12A, Cornish, 603-675-6000
*Former home of the Nichols family features permanent and rotating exhibitions and restored gardens designed by Rose Nichols.*

CURRIER GALLERY OF ART
201 Myrtle Way, Manchester, 603-669-6144
*Collection of paintings and sculpture spans 13th century to present; museum also owns and offers tours of the Zimmerman House by Frank Lloyd Wright.*

ENFIELD SHAKER VILLAGE
Rte. 4A, Enfield, 603-632-4346
*Museum and workshop document and perpetuate Shaker handcraft traditions.*

HOOD MUSEUM OF ART
Wheelock St., Hanover, 603-646-2808
*Dartmouth College museum is among nation's oldest and largest college museums.*

MOUNT KEARSARGE INDIAN MUSEUM
Kearsarge Mountain Rd., Warner, 603-456-2600
*Large collection of mostly 19th- and 20th-century Native American trade items, with focus on New England and eastern Canadian tribes.*

MUSEUM OF NEW HAMPSHIRE HISTORY
Eagle Sq., Concord, 603-226-3189
*Early New Hampshire furniture, one of the finest surviving Concord coaches, Native American artifacts.*

NEW HAMPSHIRE SNOWMOBILE MUSEUM
Bear Brook State Park, Allenstown, 603-271-3254
*Collection of vintage snowmobiles.*

STRAWBERY BANKE MUSEUM
Marcy St., Portsmouth, 603-433-1100
*Documents four centuries of Portsmouth architecture and domestic life in villagelike setting.*

## Attractions

CHRISTA MCAULIFFE PLANETARIUM
3 Institute Dr., Concord, 603-271-7827
*State-of-the-art domed theater introduces the wonder of space.*

FORT AT NO. 4
Springfield Rd., Charlestown, 603-826-5700
*Re-creates northernmost outpost of the frontier between New England and New France from 1740–60.*

MOUNT WASHINGTON AUTO ROAD
Rte. 16, Gorham, 603-466-3988
*Eight-mile road to the summit of Mt. Washington.*

MOUNT WASHINGTON COG RAILWAY
Rte. 302, Bretton Woods, 603-278-5404
*One of the steepest tracks in the world for colorful ride to the summit.*

M/S MOUNT WASHINGTON
Town docks, Wolfeboro and Weirs Beach, 603-366-2628
*Historic steamboat cruises on Lake Winnipesaukee.*

STATE HOUSE AND VISITORS' CENTER
107 N. Main St., Concord, 603-271-2154
*Self-guided tours of state house.*

WEATHER DISCOVERY CENTER
Rte. 16, North Conway, 603-356-2137
*Interactive exhibits introduce scientific concepts about weather observation and provide information about observatory on Mt. Washington summit.*

WHITE MOUNTAIN NATIONAL FOREST
719 Main St., Laconia, 603-528-8721, TTY 603-528-8722
*The 780,000-acre forest is the largest tract of public land in New England; more than 5,000 miles of hiking trails.*

## Homes and Gardens

DANIEL WEBSTER BIRTHPLACE
Off Rte. 127, Franklin, 603-934-5057
*Two-room frame house, built in 1782, contains period furnishings.*

FRANKLIN PIERCE HOMESTEAD
Rtes. 9 & 31, Hillsborough, 603-478-3165
*The 1804 mansion was the childhood home of the 14th president.*

FROST PLACE
Ridge Rd., Franconia, 603-823-5510
*Robert Frost's farm is now a museum and center for the arts.*

FULLER GARDENS
10 Willow Ave., North Hampton, 603-964-5414
*Early 20th-century estate garden features 2,000-plus rosebushes and Japanese garden.*

GOVERNOR JOHN LANGDON HOUSE
143 Pleasant St., Portsmouth, 603-436-3205
*Georgian-style mansion built in 1784.*

JACKSON HOUSE
76 Northwest St., Portsmouth, 603-436-3205
*Oldest house in New Hampshire; built in 1664.*

JOHN PAUL JONES HOUSE
43 Middle St., Portsmouth, 603-436-8420
*Former sea captain's home turned boarding house, best known for its most famous boarder.*

MOFFATT-LADD HOUSE
154 Market St., Portsmouth, 603-436-1118
*Mansion completed in 1763 has extensive gardens.*

RHODODENDRON STATE PARK
Fitzwilliam, 603-532-8862
*More than 16 acres of rhododendrons, one of the largest plantings north of the Allegheny Mountains, bloom in mid-July.*

ROBERT FROST HOMESTEAD
Rte. 28, Derry, 603-432-3091
*Frost lived here from 1901–1909.*

RUNDLET-MAY HOUSE
364 Middle St., Portsmouth, 603-436-3205
*Early 19th-century home had all the latest conveniences, circa 1810.*

SAINT-GAUDENS NATIONAL HISTORIC SITE
Cornish, 603-675-2175
*Home and studio of Augustus Saint-Gaudens is now a national park.*

WARNER HOUSE
150 Daniel St., Portsmouth, 603-436-5909
*Georgian mansion built in 1716 contains some of the oldest murals in the country.*

WENTWORTH-GARDNER HOUSE
50 Mechanic St., Portsmouth, 603-436-4406
*Small Georgian mansion, once owned and restored by Wallace Nutting.*

## Other Resources

ART GALLERY, UNIVERSITY OF NEW HAMPSHIRE
Paul Creative Arts Center, Durham, 603-862-3712
*Changing exhibitions of historical to contemporary fine arts and crafts.*

THE BALSAMS
Rte. 16, Dixville Notch, 603-255-3400
*One of the last grand White Mountain resort hotels.*

BARNSTORMERS
Main St., Tamworth, 603-323-8500
*Venerable summer theater company near Lake Winnipesaukee.*

CAPITOL CENTER FOR THE ARTS
44 South Main St., Concord, 603-225-1111
*Leading performing arts venue of the Merrimack Valley.*

HOPKINS CENTER
Dartmouth College campus, Hanover, 603-646-2422
*Major performance venue for dance, theater, and music.*

LAKES REGION SUMMER THEATER
Rte. 25, Meredith, 603-279-9933
*Summer theater on Lake Winnipesaukee.*

LEAGUE OF NEW HAMPSHIRE CRAFTSMEN SHOPS
36 North Main St., Concord, 603-228-8171
61 Water St., Exeter, 603-778-8282
13 Lebanon St., Hanover, 603-643-5050
279 Daniel Webster Hwy., Meredith, 603-279-7920

Main St., Center Sandwich, 603-284-6831
64 Center St., Wolfeboro Falls, 603-569-3309
2526 Main St., North Conway, 603-356-2441
*Shops stock a juried selection of traditional and contemporary fine crafts.*

MOUNT WASHINGTON HOTEL & RESORT
Rte. 302, Bretton Woods, 603-278-1000
*One of the last grand White Mountain resort hotels.*

MOUNT WASHINGTON VALLEY THEATRE COMPANY
Eastern Slope Playhouse, North Conway, 603-356-5776
*Summer theater in the White Mountains.*

NEW HAMPSHIRE ART ASSOCIATION ROBERT LINCOLN LEVY GALLERY
136 State St., Portsmouth, 603-431-4230
*Juried exhibitions of artist members.*

NEW HAMPSHIRE INSTITUTE OF ART
148 Concord St., Manchester, 603-623-0313
*State's only freestanding art school has gallery of changing exhibitions.*

NEW LONDON PLAYHOUSE
209 Main St., New London, 603-526-4631
*Summer theater at Lake Sunapee.*

PETERBOROUGH PLAYERS
Hadley Rd., Peterborough, 603-924-7585
*Summer theater in the Monadnock region.*

# CREDITS

The authors have made every effort to reach copyright holders of text and owners of illustrations, and wish to thank those individuals and institutions that permitted the reprinting of text or the reproduction of works in their collections. Credits not listed in the captions are provided below. References are to page numbers; the designations a, b, and c indicate position of illustrations on pages.

## Text

Beacon Press: From *Last House on the Road: Excursions Into a Rural Past* by Ronald Jager. Copyright © 1994 by Ronald Jager.

Graywolf Press: Excerpts from "Mud Season" and "Ice Out" from *Otherwise: New and Selected Poems* by Jane Kenyon. Copyright © 1996 by Jane Kenyon. Used by permission of Graywolf Press.

Donald Hall and Houghton Mifflin Company: Excerpts from *Here at Eagle Pond* by Donald Hall. Copyright © 1990 by Donald Hall.

Henry Holt & Co., Inc.: Lines from "Mending Wall," from *The Poetry of Robert Frost*, edited by Edward Connery Lathem. Copyright © 1958, 1962 by Robert Frost. Copyright © 1967, 1970 by Lesley Frost Ballantine. Copyright © 1930, 1939, © 1969 by Henry Holt & Company.

Mekeel McBride and Carnegie Mellon University Press: Excerpt from "Growing Stones in New Hampshire" from *Red Letter Days* by Mekeel McBride. Copyright © 1988 by Mekeel McBride.

Random House, Inc.: From *Simple Gifts: A Memoir of a Shaker Village* by June Sprigg. Copyright © 1998 by June Sprigg. Reprinted by permission of Alfred A. Knopf, a division of Random House, Inc.

W. W. Norton & Co., Inc.: From *New England Flavor: Memories*

*of a Country Boyhood* by Haydn S. Pearson. Copyright © 1961 by Haydn S. Pearson. Reprinted by permission of W. W. Norton & Co., Inc.

## Illustrations

ABBY ALDRICH ROCKEFELLER FOLK ART CENTER, WILLIAMS-BURG, VA.: **9** *The Tilton Family.* Watercolor, pencil, and ink on woven paper. 10 x 15⅛". 1936.300.6; COURTESY AMERICA'S STONEHENGE: **86a**; ART SHOWS AND PRODUCTS: **19** *The River at Ascutney.* Oil on panel. 23 x 18½". Photo courtesy Archives of the American Illustrators Gallery, New York City. © 2000 ASaP of Holderness, NH 03245, USA, Authorized by the Maxfield Parrish Family Trust; BANK OF NEW HAMPSHIRE/MCGOWAN FINE ART: **84b** *Icon for the Musical Rations of Nature.* Oil and gold leaf on wood. 27¼ x 36"; BEADLESTON GALLERY: **21** *Sun Setting onto Fog.* Oil on canvas. 36 x 52". © Wolf Kahn/Licensed by VAGA, New York, NY; DAVID BROWNELL: **15a**; CHRISTIE'S IMAGES: **40a** *Picking up the Pilot—Isle of Shoals, New Hampshire.* Oil on canvas. 17 x 27"; CULVER PICTURES: **39**; CURRIER GALLERY OF ART, MANCHESTER: **34** *Plowing the Fields.* Oil on canvas. 24 x 36". Gift of Dr. and Mrs. R. Huntington Breed II, Mrs. Elenore Freedman, the Friends, Mr. and Mrs. Saul Greenspan, Mr. and Mrs. James W. Griswold, Mr. and Mrs. Robert C. Holcombe, Mr. and Mrs. John F. Swope, Mr. and Mrs. Davis P. Thurber, and Mr. and Mrs. Kimon S. Zachos. Photo by Bill Finney; **58** *Chest on chest frame.* Maple and pine. 82⅝ x 41⅛ x 20". Currier Funds. 1959.3. Photo by Bill Finney; DAN DAILEY: **84a** *Ram-Headed Man.* Handblown glass, patina, gold plate, and beads. 15½ x 12¾ x 10". Photo by Bill Truslow; JOHN HATCH: **85** *Hawthorn Twig.* Oil on canvas. 30 x 22⅜"; ROBERT HOLMES/CORBIS: **89**; HOOD MUSEUM OF ART, DARTMOUTH COLLEGE, HANOVER, N.H.: **26** *Indian Hunter with Bow.* Pastel on sanded paper. 43.8 cm x 52.8 cm. Pur-